Berthe
Morisot

By Anne Higonnet

RIZZOLI ART SERIES

Series Editor: Norma Broude

Berthe

Morisot

(1841–1895)

BERTHE MORISOT was one of the founders of Impressionism and remained one of its eight principal members. She, Edgar Degas, Claude Monet, Alfred Sisley, Camille Pissarro, and Auguste Renoir launched the painting movement that was to become one of the world's most beloved; they were soon joined by Gustave Caillebotte and Mary Cassatt. Never before in the history of art had women played artistic roles so innovative and so influential. Morisot's achievements were all the more remarkable because she remained rooted in middle-class feminine traditions of picture making that were not obviously compatible with elite artistic standards, and because she lived a personal life that in some ways was also conventionally middleclass and feminine. Astute adjustments and compromises, as well as an iron will and exceptional pictorial talents, enabled Morisot to reconcile the demands of femininity with those of an outstanding career. Morisot began her lifework constrained both by rules of art and rules of gender. By the time she died, at the age of fifty-four in 1895, she had altered those rules for herself and for others.

In letters and diaries, as well as in conversations with family and peers, Morisot disclaimed any professional and artistic ambitions. Throughout her life she was her own severest critic, constantly belittling her paintings and their place in art history. Early in her career, facing the prospect of an exhibition, she "preferred to be at the bottom of a river than to learn her painting had been accepted."[1] Decades later, when she was much more experienced and had received all kinds of accolades, she still could write: "I hate everything I've done," and, "the desire for glorification after death seems to me an unreasonable ambition. Mine is limited to wanting to *capture something that passes*; oh, just something! the least of things."[2]

Yet at the same time that she was writing such disparaging remarks about herself and her painting, she was not only steadily producing innovative work but also reforming her profession. Not content with the rewards of solitary creation, she worked to reform the public art world. During her youth, that world was dominated by French state institutions all located in Paris: a school, an exhibition forum, and an academy that governed both school and exhibition, called, respectively, the Ecole des Beaux-Arts, the Salon, and the Académie des Beaux-Arts. These institutions officially promoted large-scale paintings of mythological, historical, or religious subjects and only applauded a very finely brushed, optically realistic style so smooth it was called

léché, meaning "licked." In the early 1870s, a group of young painters decided to challenge this system. They resolved to exhibit their paintings independently, assuming all the risks, and, of course, hoping to reap all the profits. They were very much in the latest spirit of venture capitalists, which at the time was the least controversial aspect of their enterprise. Most of them were solidly middle-class, and they appealed directly to a middle-class audience by painting subjects drawn from their common daily life, by scaling down their paintings to hang on apartment walls, and by charging prices individuals (as opposed to institutions) could afford. Their exhibitions, known collectively as the Impressionist exhibitions, introduced the Parisian public to a style of art that eventually won immense popularity. From the very start, critics commented on the extraordinary fact that among the leaders of the new movement there was a woman—Berthe Morisot.

Critics of course commented on many other aspects of the movement as well, and not often favorably. Most people, even in sophisticated Parisian circles, at first resisted Impressionism, bewildered by its many innovations. As if it weren't enough to propose a new kind of organization, new financing, a new scale, and new subjects, the Impressionists' paintings were also executed in a style that previously had been considered suitable only for sketches, never for "finished" paintings. One critic reacted by derisively labeling the young group "Impressionist," a name Morisot and her friends proceeded defiantly to adopt. Morisot may have had doubts about herself, but they did not prevent her from withstanding both hostile criticism from the outside and the tensions among the Impressionists that hostility caused. Much more worrisome to her than other people's opinions of her own painting were negative descriptions of her colleagues' work. She believed in the kind of painting she practiced, and she was deeply loyal to her fellow Impressionists, even if she questioned the value of her own contributions.

Morisot could not meet the young male painters of her generation professionally since no major art school or studio then accepted women. But she did have the good fortune to be born into a family that allowed her to meet her peers socially. Her father was a high-level civil servant, and her mother entertained regularly—perhaps at her daughter's request, she frequently invited young people in the arts as well as in politics and government. The Morisots were then invited in return. Thus between about 1865 and 1870 Berthe met the ambitious young men who were becoming convinced that they should devote their painting to the representation of modern life. Some, such as Henri Fantin-Latour, Alfred Stevens, and James Tissot, wanted to do so and still use a conservative style that could win them favor from traditional patrons and from the Académie des Beaux-Arts. Others, including Frédéric Bazille, Degas, Monet, and Renoir, thought that new subjects demanded a new way of painting, which they were still tentatively developing. One, Edouard Manet, had already become a notorious pioneer of the new painting. Despite the revolutionary impact on the Parisian art world of his masterpieces *Olympia* and *Luncheon on the Grass* (first shown in 1863 and 1865), however, he yearned for official acceptance. Although he remained on excellent terms with most of his followers and continued to inspire them, he would never join them in their rebellion against existing institutions. Manet was the painter with

1. Edouard Manet. *The Balcony*. c.1869–1870.
Oil on canvas, 66½ × 48 ⅜". Musée d'Orsay,
Paris. Giraudon/Art Resource, New York

2. Edouard Manet. *Berthe Morisot with a
Bouquet of Violets*. 1872. Oil on canvas,
21⅝ × 14⅞". Private collection, Paris.
Giraudon/Art Resource, New York

whom Morisot had the closest personal relationship. They shared exactly the same social background, and from the first time she saw his work, Morisot believed Manet was the greatest painter of his time. He in turn admired her very individual elegance as well as her painting, and he asked her to model for some of his finest works, including *The Balcony* (fig. 1) and *Berthe Morisot with a Bouquet of Violets* (fig. 2). Nonetheless—and contrary to what art historians maintained for more than a century—Morisot was more influenced professionally by Degas, because Degas urged her to paint as she wished to, and because it was he who, arguing directly against Manet, convinced Morisot to participate with him in the dissident exhibition of 1874.

Her allegiance to Impressionism proved durable. Morisot invested herself completely in the movement: artistically, financially, and socially. Her commitment to the Impressionists' success not only led her to help organize and pay for the last of their group exhibitions, but also to cultivate the bonds among the original Impressionists, which were often strained during the early years by public indifference and hostility. She extended professional relationships into personal friendships. Always cordial with Pissarro and Sisley, she developed very close ties to Monet and especially to Renoir, whom she saw regularly for the rest of her life. After Mary Cassatt, also encouraged by Degas, joined the Impressionists in 1879, Morisot could match herself against another woman. The two women Impressionists were always friends, and even briefly worked together on the same subject, just as Monet and Renoir had painted side by side. Yet like many artists who work within the same territory, Cassatt and Morisot also felt a certain rivalry between them, which expressed itself constructively in formal experimentation and a heightened desire to gain public recognition through exhibition.

Altogether, the Impressionists held eight exhibitions over a period of twelve years. Morisot abstained from one, probably because that year, 1879, the recent birth of her only child, Julie, had prevented her from producing much new work. Morisot had married Edouard Manet's younger brother Eugène not long after the first exhibition, which of

course reinforced her social ties among the circle of avant-garde painters. As she grew older, her network broadened to include notable sculptors, politicians, and writers, especially the poet Stéphane Mallarmé, who became a close friend, particularly after the death of her husband in 1892. When Morisot died in 1895, Mallarmé, together with Degas, Monet, and Renoir, organized a posthumous retrospective of her work, for which Mallarmé wrote an extremely perceptive catalogue essay. Her friends had reciprocated her solidarity, proving what Pissarro wrote after she died, that "she did honor to our Impressionist group."[3]

Morisot had participated in every aspect of the group, including its very modern appreciation of painting technique. Nowadays, the short, thick, individual brushstrokes with which the Impressionists conveyed their vision have become so familiar that we completely accept their calligraphic flourish and brilliant color and hardly notice how artful they are. Impressionist paintings seem to be so natural, so spontaneous, that they lull us into forgetting their style's calculated effects. Morisot chose subjects of great significance to herself and other women, and she used technique to represent those subjects in unprecedented and thought-provoking ways. Like her most daring peers, though, she was also fascinated with technique for its own sake. She was perhaps the first woman in the history of art to locate her artistic identity in style, a fundamentally modern concept that eventually dominated the high arts. Such celebrated women artists as Elisabeth Vigée-Lebrun or Rosa Bonheur had been accomplished practitioners of established styles that subordinated themselves to their subject matter. Cassatt, in 1890 and 1891, did conduct bold stylistic experiments in her color prints. But Morisot had the courage, or the ego, to make her individuality permeate the way she applied oil pigments to canvas. She embedded a stylistic signature in every tiny choice she made about color, composition, and brushwork.

Morisot liked to play with spatial illusions and asymmetric compositions. Unmediated contrasts between the apparently very close and very far recur throughout her work. *View of Paris from the Trocadéro* (plate 11) offers us one of Morisot's few spatially continuous landscapes. In a more typical picture, *Interior at the Isle of Wight* (plate 5), Eugène Manet seems to sit quite close to us, while between the window sashes we glimpse the port across a promenade. In other pictures a small window at the edge directs our gaze to a street or a garden. To construct her spaces, Morisot frequently balanced uneven distributions of pictorial elements both from back to front and from side to side, as she did in *Boats on the Seine* (plate 12), where the width of the boat in the right foreground lines up exactly below a block of clustered houses in the right background, and the black rim of the boat also echoes the bridge that stretches across the river from the left. Rationally we know the bridge should be diagonal, but Morisot convincingly and cleverly represents it as almost parallel to the boat, and just about as far from the top edge of her canvas as the boat rim is from the bottom edge. Like so many seemingly casual Impressionist landscapes, Morisot's have in fact been carefully planned to provide the sense of structure that makes any work of fiction satisfying.

These compositional effects were all the more difficult to achieve because Morisot chose to work almost exclusively with color and hardly at all with line. She did draw regularly, and occasionally she would prepare a painting with many sketches, but generally she went directly to the canvas with palette and brush. Not only did she work expressively with black (plates 1, 3, 14), but she also accomplished rare pictorial feats with bright, light colors. She dared to construct spatial illusions with colors quite similar to one another in terms of light and dark. Look for instance at *The Quay at Bougival* (plate 9). At close range, or in a black-and-white reproduction, the painting appears to be an almost random scattering of marks. As you step farther back from the painting, however, or if you look at a good color reproduction, all those marks resolve themselves into a very strong impression of three-dimensional space: an expanse of water, a flight of steps, a vertical embankment, an invisible street with houses on the other side. Only the optical differences of hue hold those illusions together. Although in her earlier years Morisot used color most boldly in her landscape pictures, toward the end of her career she began to suffuse even her large-scale figure paintings with high-key color, as she did in her *Cherry Pickers* (plate 13); the girl on the ladder seems to glow from within just as the sun shines through the foliage around her.

Most idiosyncratically, Morisot liked to push technique to its limits to imply emotional meanings. Even more than her fellow Impressionists, Morisot intentionally left all or parts of her canvases covered with what at the time were perceived as sketches rather than finished paintings. In her *Self-Portrait* (plate 10) Morisot put the bare minimum needed to convey the image of a face on the sheet of paper. The right eye is just one thick black pastel mark; the nose, indicated only by its shadows. Technically, this is Morisot displaying her skill, showing how little she needs to do to make a recognizable self-portrait. Expressively, she uses that skill to convey her feelings about her sense of an inner reality. Her face looks as if it were being wiped away, as if its substance might only be a passing illusion. The art historian Linda Nochlin has admired the eloquence of Morisot's technique in her late work *Julie Manet and Her Greyhound* (plate 14), drawing our attention to the extremely sketchy chair at the left and suggesting that its virtual transparency

evokes the recent death of Eugène Manet, father of the person in the painting, husband of the one who makes the painting. His is the empty place, the vanishing place, the loss in the image of the family.[4] Yet Morisot's skill also allowed her to depict a feeling or an attitude with unusually dense brushwork rather than remarkably thin strokes. In *The Cradle* (plate 4), for example, by far the heaviest marks on the canvas are those that indicate a pink ribbon threaded along the edge of the cradle's veil. We know that, for strictly representational purposes, the ribbon does not need to seem any heavier than the mother's dress, certainly not heavier than the bodies of the mother and baby. But the heaviness of the ribbon conveys Morisot's idea of a boundary between the mother and her child, a line that separates them and makes them two individuals.

In *The Cradle*, the mother communicates her tenderness by the way she looks at her baby. Morisot had declined more common sentimental or physical signs of affection. She often pictured people in the act of looking, perhaps more often than she pictured them doing anything else. After all, she was someone whose profession was based on looking, and whose technique expressed her fascination with the ways in which materials—oils, pastels, or watercolors—could translate the emotional and intellectual as well as the physiological nuances of observation. Morisot made looking the subject of her art in three ways, each represented among this book's illustrations. Besides *The Cradle*, three other paintings show people absorbed in looking: the title of *View of Paris from the Trocadéro* (plate 11) tells us that the two women in the foreground have come to look at Paris from a famous vantage point (the same spot tourists now visit to look at the Eiffel Tower); Eugène Manet in his 1875 portrait (plate 5) is amusing himself by looking out the window; while the woman in *Lady at Her Toilette* (plate 8) is looking at herself in her mirror. In Morisot's *Self-Portrait* (plate 10), we assume she too is looking at herself in a mirror, although the effect is that she is looking very hard at us. In many of Morisot's strongest works, such as the *Self-Portrait*, the sitter and the painter gaze steadily at each other, so that we are confronted with some of the most direct looks from women in the history of painting up to that time. The woman in *Daydreaming* (plate 7) may be looking right past us, but the gazes of Morisot's sister Edma Morisot Pontillon in her portrait (plate 3) and Julie's in hers (plate 14) rivet us with their intensity. Morisot also included in some of these paintings and in many others references to, or emblems of, sight: mirrors (plates 1 and 8), windows (plates 4, 5, and 7), and works of art within her works of art (plates 2 and 14). They remind us to think about how we see what we look at.

Morisot achieved her professional status and acquired her technical skills against tremendous odds. She was one of the very few women before the middle of this century who managed to become an eminent and influential artist. Because she was obliged to overcome so many obstacles other than purely artistic challenges in order to become an artist, Morisot's career shows us how contemporary ideas about art functioned within a much broader set of ideas about masculine and feminine roles as well as about social class, and how those cultural concepts changed during the nineteenth century.

Consider Morisot's portraits by Manet (for example figs. 1 and 2). In these images Morisot fulfills our traditional expectations of femininity. She is beautiful, well-groomed, elegantly dressed, and quietly posed. Setting and costume tell us furthermore that she belongs to the upper middle class of French society, which in the nineteenth century was basically the class that all other classes emulated, particularly as regards femininity. Of course she also looks extremely intelligent, but this too was an aspect of a progressively traditional ideal of "Woman," as long as a woman's intelligence was confined to matrimony, maternity, philanthropy, and possibly entertainment. Nothing in Manet's portraits of Morisot indicates the contrary. Looking at them, you would never know that she too was a painter. But she was. She turned gender roles around and went from being the muse to being the one who creates, from being the one who is looked at to being the one who looks.

Manet's portraits of Morisot also show us, however, that she did not trade one set of stereotypes for another. All her life, in every way, Morisot balanced aspects of her behavior so that she could be accepted socially and professionally. She cultivated the personal appearance that Manet admired so much, and was proud of it. She married happily, entertained graciously, and devoted herself passionately to her child. Other members of her family sometimes resented what they perceived as her frigid reserve and dauntingly high standards, which in retrospect we can see were the inevitable consequences of a woman making herself so regularly unavailable both emotionally and physically because she spent so much time working or socializing with colleagues. Even such friends as Mallarmé, who once called her a "friendly Medusa," were a bit cowed by her self-control and her rigorous taste. Yet except in a few moments confided to her rare surviving private notebooks, Morisot never explicitly rebelled against any social conventions.

Even the subject matter of Morisot's paintings at first appears deceptively docile. Almost all the women in Morisot's images are like Manet's images of her: well-bred and well behaved. They occupy the sites of middle-class feminine leisure: sitting rooms, boudoirs, parks, and gardens. Their immaculate costumes indicate the quiet intimacy of Morisot's moments, removed from the agitation of the outside, commercial, masculine world. On first glance, Morisot's women seem quintessentially feminine and private, and her exclusive attention to them seems to confirm her own private femininity. She painted the women in her family more than anyone else; her sisters Edma (plates 1, 2, 3, and 4) and Yves, her mother (plate 1), her nieces (plate 4), her daughter most of all (plates 6 and 14). Morisot almost never painted men, the exception being her husband (plates 5 and 6), and she almost always pictured him with their daughter. She never painted her colleagues and male friends the way Monet and Renoir painted each other, never paid tribute to Manet with a portrait the way he did to her. Moreover, Morisot painted rather small pictures, and she hardly ever made a fuss about the conditions in which she painted them, usually working in a room of a house or in the garden, sometimes in a small studio adjacent to home. Morisot stayed well within the most decorous feminine territory, avoiding the kinds of scenes that made her colleagues famous: train stations, isolated and lonely landscapes, brothels, and cafés. They felt able to paint many different subjects. She felt limited to one.

Morisot inherited the range and content of her subject matter. Since the end of the eighteenth century, middle-class women throughout Europe had practiced painting and drawing in an amateur way. They had been painting the kinds of feminine scenes that Morisot painted—the ones they encountered in lives circumscribed by gender. Women's active involvement in image making, however amateur, provided them with an experience crucial to any future professional ventures. All middle-class women by the middle of the century at least knew other women—both in their generation and in previous ones—who drew or painted, often quite well and quite consistently. Because amateur art allowed women to assume they could draw and paint, it gave them the general sense of confidence that specialized training can only build on and refine. Women's restriction of their artistic efforts to their own separate sphere, however, reinforced prevailing ideas about the gender of artistic talent. The social character of women's art was used as evidence that women were by nature unable to excel artistically. It was commonly assumed that imaginative creativity was a masculine trait. Of course the professional conditions necessary to articulate native gifts were not available to women. But the virtual absence of women in artistic professions allowed both men and women to argue that women had never been endowed with genius anyway and therefore had no need for professional opportunities. By working as amateurs, women seemed to

3. Edma Morisot. *Portrait of Berthe Morisot.* c.1865–1868. Oil on canvas, 39⅜ × 27 ⅞". Private collection

corroborate this argument. Moreover, while boundaries between amateur and professional had in the past been fluid for both men and women, during the course of the nineteenth century some kinds of art became rigidly professionalized and associated with masculinity, whereas a previously gender-neutral amateur practice became associated with femininity.

The contrast between Berthe Morisot and her sister Edma demonstrates how double-edged the amateur experience could be. Berthe and Edma took lessons together, and for twelve years they painted together. During this period, they may have been among the most accomplished and ambitious amateurs of their age, sex, and class, but they were definitely amateurs. The portrait Edma made of Berthe at the time (fig. 3) proves that the two sisters were equally talented, an opinion held by everyone who knew them. The portrait also

4. Mary Cassatt. *The Theatre Box.* c.1880. Oil on canvas, 31½ × 25 ⅛". National Gallery of Art, Washington, D.C. Chester Dale Collection, Bridgeman/Art Resource, New York

demonstrates that the sisters believed in each other as artists. Unlike Edouard Manet, Edma imagined Berthe as a painter at her easel, tools in hand, absorbed by her work. But by 1868 Edma felt she could not, or would not, cross the boundary between amateur and professional work that to women seemed implacable. She married and never painted again. Despite all social dangers, Berthe did cross that professional boundary. Amateur art had limited one sister and empowered the other.

Identical origins could produce two such different results because the art world was in confusingly rapid transition. A professional career was virtually inconceivable for women while Berthe and Edma were children. In the first half of the century, the kinds of painting that obtained high-priced commissions, secured reputations, and won academic approval demanded training in specialized schools and familiarity with classical literature, science, and history, as well as the uninterrupted time and spacious studios necessary for painstakingly detailed but vast canvases. Women were not allowed (except under very unusual circumstances) to receive such training. Only men could enroll in the most prestigious schools or studios, in particular the Ecole des Beaux-Arts. Moreover, women were not allowed to attend anatomy classes and were strongly discouraged from painting nudes, even female nudes, so that both technically and psychologically it was virtually impossible for them to produce the paintings the Académie placed at the apex of its artistic hierarchy. But as Berthe and Edma became adults, the young male painters they knew were rebelling against this hierarchy. They rejected the Académie's definitions of quality, and they did not attend the Ecole des Beaux-Arts. They insisted that smaller pictures of ordinary life could be just as important works of art as any history, religious, or mythological scene populated by nudes. They championed working out of doors, or even in home studios, and they learned as much from each other as from any teacher. So all of a sudden, exactly the kind of picture Berthe and Edma had been making became potentially professional. The training they had been denied was being declared irrelevant. In the late 1860s, though, it still required a leap of faith to think that the future Impressionists would convince

the world of their ideas. Berthe took that leap, and Edma did not. Berthe had understood that the latest trends in avant-garde art might push her socially acceptable painting just within the boundaries of elite art. To be considered a professional and yet still paint the feminine subjects she preferred, Berthe had to commit herself to the most daring art movement of her time.

Call it inconsistency or strategy. Berthe Morisot knew the value of accommodation. The situation she created for herself allowed her to enjoy both an outstanding professional career and the pleasures of marriage, maternity, and close friendships, as well as the comforts of social acceptance. More enduringly, her ability to translate the themes of femininity into professional painting enabled her to reinterpret femininity for us. True, Morisot's subjects are basically quite conventional, but the way she handled them is not. Take two relatively obvious examples, the pastel *Portrait of Edma Morisot Pontillon* (plate 3) and *Eugène Manet and His Daughter in the Garden* (plate 6). Although what we notice at first about Berthe's portrait of her sister Edma is Edma's face, if we look closely we realize that, very discreetly, Berthe has shown us by the position of Edma's hands that her sister is in the final stages of pregnancy. It was completely taboo in Morisot's time to make a portrait of an obviously pregnant woman. By breaking that taboo with such respect and affection, Morisot has given public dignity to a vital but usually hidden moment in women's lives. Or look at Morisot's portrait of her husband and child. Eugène Manet is taking care of Julie while Morisot works. The usual roles of mother

5. Edgar Degas. *Madame Théodore Gobillard (Yves Morisot, 1838–1893).* Oil on canvas, 25⅝ × 21⅜". The Metropolitan Museum of Art, New York. H. O. Havemeyer Collection, Bequest of Mrs. H. O. Havemeyer, 1929 (29.100.45)

and father have been reversed, but again with deference and tenderness. Father and daughter play the same game, placed so that the mother could join from her side at any moment. In Morisot's image, the members of the family are equals.

Morisot's art unfolded over the course of a long career. Self-expression requires more than a natural gift; it also depends on the acquired accomplishments of disciplined thought, years of technical experience, the competition as well as the support of colleagues, and the criticism of a public audience. Morisot was blessed with the gift, and, against all odds, won for herself the accomplishments. She used them well. Look at the differences between her very early and very late works, between her portrait of her mother and sister made in 1869–1870 (plate 1) when Morisot was twenty-eight or twenty-nine, and her portrait of her daughter made in 1893, only two years before her death (plate 14). In a superficial way, nothing has changed; both pictures show seated women similarly placed in the shallow spaces of parlors. The earlier picture is famous in art history for a dubious reason; as Morisot herself and her mother told the story in letters, Edouard Manet took it upon himself to help Morisot at the last minute before submission of the work to the Salon by repainting parts of the figure on the right. Morisot was angry but it was too late to correct the corrections. Furthermore, the painting had originally been directly inspired by a portrait that Degas had made of Berthe's other sister Yves (fig. 5), using the same setting, merely shifted to one side. By the end of her career, Morisot did not depend on masculine inspiration or assistance and felt free to use the same basic idea in a much more original way. Her brushwork, once tightly diffident, had become individual and expressive. The earlier picture conveys a feeling of confinement and restraint; the mother blocks access to her daughter, and the two women do not communicate with each other. The daughter, her pregnancy muffled in clothing, has abandoned her dreams and entered into the cycle of passive femininity that will make her like her mother. Her gaze wanders, unfocused. The only escape comes symbolically, within the framed image on the wall, a mirror that reflects a tiny bit of open window between heavy curtains. Twenty-three years later, Morisot's vision of women has changed. Here too there is sadness, in the empty chair and the young woman's mourning dress, but we are invited to share it by the greyhound who directs our gaze into the painting's space. The daughter, sensual yet unselfconscious, leans forward, clear-eyed, toward her mother, toward us, toward the world around her.

NOTES

(For short citations, refer to Further Reading)

1. Higonnet, *Berthe Morisot*, p. 64.
2. Ibid., p. 203.
3. Camille Pissarro, *Lettres à Lucien*, ed. Lucien Pissarro and John Rewald (Paris: Albin Michel, 1950), p. 371, n. 6.
4. Nochlin, "Morisot's Wet Nurse," p. 52.

FURTHER READING

Adler, Kathleen, and Tamar Garb. *Berthe Morisot*. Ithaca, N.Y.: Cornell University Press, 1987.

Bataille, Marie-Louise, and Georges Wildenstein. *Berthe Morisot: Catalogue des peintures, pastels, et aquarelles*. Paris: Wildenstein, 1961.

Broude, Norma. *Impressionism, A Feminist Reading: The Gendering of Art, Science, and Nature in the Nineteenth Century*. New York: Rizzoli, 1991.

Edelstein, T. J., ed. *Perspectives on Morisot*. New York: Hudson Hills Press, in association with the Mount Holyoke College Art Museum, 1990.

Herbert, Robert L. *Impressionism: Art, Leisure, and Parisian Society*. New Haven, Conn.: Yale University Press, 1988.

Higonnet, Anne. *Berthe Morisot*. New York: Harper & Row, 1990.

————. *Berthe Morisot's Images of Women*. Cambridge, Mass.: Harvard University Press, 1992.

Huisman, Philippe. *Morisot: Charmes*. Lausanne: International Art Books, 1962.

Mallarmé, Stéphane. "Berthe Morisot." In *Oeuvres complètes*, pp. 533–537. Paris: Gallimard, 1961.

Manet, Julie. *Journal (1893–1899)*. Paris: Klincksieck, 1979.

Morisot, Berthe. *Correspondance*, ed. Denis Rouart. 1957. Reprint. Mt. Kisco, N.Y.: Moyer Bell Limited, 1986.

Nochlin, Linda. "Morisot's Wet Nurse." In *Women, Art, and Power and Other Essays*, pp. 37–56. New York: Harper & Row, 1988.

Pollock, Griselda. "Modernity and the Spaces of Femininity." In *Vision and Difference: Femininity, Feminism, and the Histories of Art*, pp. 50–90. London and New York: Routledge, 1988.

Rey, Jean-Dominique. *Berthe Morisot*. 2d ed. Paris: Flammarion, 1989.

Stuckey, Charles F., William P. Scott, and Suzanne Lindsay. *Berthe Morisot: Impressionist*. New York: Hudson Hills Press, 1987.

First published in 1993 in the United States of America by Rizzoli International Publications, Inc.
300 Park Avenue South
New York, New York 10010

Library of Congress Cataloging-in-Publication Data
Higonnet, Anne.
    Berthe Morisot/by Anne Higonnet.
        p.   cm. — (Rizzoli art series)
    Includes bibliographical references and index.
    ISBN 0-8478-1646-X
    1. Morisot, Berthe. 1841–1895—Criticism and interpretation.
    I. Title.   II. Series.
    ND553.M88H5   1993
    759.4—dc20   92-36278
                                                  CIP

Series Editor: Norma Broude

Series designed by José Conde and Betty Lew/Rizzoli
Editor: Charles Miers; Assistant Editor: Jennifer Condon

Printed in Italy

Front cover: See colorplate 4

Index to Colorplates

1. *Portrait of the Artist's Mother and Sister*. 1869–1870. This painting was Morisot's largest early figure painting. She devoted her efforts to showing her mother reading, seated near her sister, in the family living room. Edma has returned to her parents' home to await the birth of her first child.

2. *The Sisters*. 1869. Behind her two figures, Morisot has placed a picture-within-a-picture, a fan painting by Degas. She thus pays tribute to his influence on her. Yet the similarity between this painting of Morisot's and paintings by Cassatt (fig. 4) shows us that the women Impressionists used their male colleagues' support to explore new territory of their own. Cassatt, like Morisot, explores the subtle differences between seemingly identical women, while Morisot contrasts Degas's artificial fan on the wall with the functional fan one sister holds, Cassatt places a deceptive mirror behind her figures that confuses our perception of their space.

3. *Portrait of Edma Morisot Pontillon*. 1871. Here Morisot used her crayons to create a smooth black expanse of clothing and brightly stylized background that contrast dramatically with the sensitively detailed portrait of her sister's face and the delicate evocations of Edma's hands, crossed protectively over her unborn child.

4. *The Cradle*. 1872. This picture, which has become Morisot's most famous, portrays Edma again, now with her second child. It was shown at the first of the Impressionist exhibitions in 1874. Rarely is the relationship of a new mother with her baby handled so unsentimentally and yet so tenderly.

5. *Interior at the Isle of Wight*. 1875. Morisot made this portrait of her husband during their honeymoon. Eugène Manet supported his wife's painting career in every way, but Morisot did complain jokingly that he was a recalcitrant model.

6. *Eugène Manet and His Daughter at Bougival*. 1883. Morisot's pictures convey moods but never tell any particular story. She could have turned the image of a father and daughter into a moralistic or edifying tale, but chose instead to capture a still moment in which both figures are enigmatically absorbed in their own thoughts.

7. *Daydreaming*. 1877. Reclining in a peignoir and slippers, this young woman relaxes before she appears in public. In most contemporary pictures of a similar theme, the artist would have emphasized the woman's sexuality. Morisot chooses a more discreet treatment, which conceals the woman's body beneath her clothing, and places the picture's emphasis on the head positioned against the bright curtains.

8. *Lady at Her Toilette*. c.1875. Here the woman takes a last look in the mirror before she goes out for the evening. We do not see her face, even in the mirror, but we sense her concentration on her image. Very unusually, Morisot has signed her name in a significant place, along the bottom of the mirror, rather than in the usual bottom right-hand corner of the canvas. She seems to be likening to her own painting the mirror into which the woman looks.

9. *The Quay at Bougival*. 1883. For two years Morisot lived in the Parisian suburb of Bougival. The town inspired a number of paintings, remarkably free in their rendition of light, color, and space.

10. *Self-Portrait*. c.1885. In 1885 Morisot made three self-portraits, all in the same clothing and therefore apparently at the same time, but each presenting quite a different self-image. This is the most disturbing of the trio. None were intended for public exhibition; Morisot concealed them, and they were only discovered after her death.

11. *View of Paris from the Trocadéro*. 1872. The scene takes place in Morisot's neighborhood, called Passy. Barely five minutes from her home, two elegantly dressed and unaccompanied young women have come to enjoy the view of central Paris across the Seine. Morisot shows the silhouettes of several major monuments on her skyline, including Nôtre-Dame, the Invalides, and the Champ-de-Mars.

12. *Boats on the Seine*. c.1880. Like many Impressionist landscapes, this one shows a suburb of Paris along the river Seine. The suburb is manifestly new, with its modern villas, iron bridge, and pleasure boats. Morisot's preference for modernity extended itself from subjects, to style, to the places she chose to live.

13. *The Cherry Pickers*. 1891. Of all her paintings, this is the one Morisot worked on the hardest. She actually made two versions of it, after many preparatory studies. Having sold the final product, she regretted her action and bought the painting back from the dealer so that she could bequeath it to her daughter.

14. *Julie Manet and Her Greyhound*. 1893. Morisot's daughter, Julie, became her favorite painting subject. During the last fifteen years of her life, Morisot made dozens of portraits of Julie. The result is the most extensive and innovative exploration of the mother-daughter relationship in the history of art to date.

1. *Portrait of the Artist's Mother and Sister.* 1869–1870. Oil on canvas, 39¾ × 32⅛"
National Gallery of Art, Washington, D.C. Chester Dale Collection

2. *The Sisters.* 1869. Oil on canvas, 20½ × 32".

3. *Portrait of Edma Morisot Pontillon.* 1871. Pastel on paper, 31⅞ × 25½".
Musée d'Orsay, Paris. ©Photo R.M.N.

4. *The Cradle.* 1872. Oil on canvas, 20 × 16⅛". Musée d'Orsay, Paris.
©Photo R.M.N.

6. *Eugène Manet and His Daughter at Bougival.* 1883. Oil on canvas, 23⅝ × 28¾".
Private collection, Paris. Giraudon/Art Resource, New York

7 *Daydreaming*, 1877. Pastel on canvas, 19⅛ x 24⅝". The Newark Museum, Gift of Mrs. ... C. ... M. ...

8. *Lady at Her Toilette.* c.1875. Oil on canvas, 23¾ × 31⅝". The Art Institute of Chicago, Stickney Fund, 1924.127.

9. *The Quay at Bougival.* 1883. Oil on canvas, 21⅞ × 18⅛". ©Nasjonalgalleriet, Oslo.
Photograph by Jacques Lathion

10. *Self-Portrait.* c.1885. Pastel, with stumping, on gray laid paper with blue fibers, 18⅞ × 14⅞".
The Art Institute of Chicago, Regenstein Collection, 1965.685 recto. Photograph ©1992,

11. *View of Paris from the Trocadéro,* 1872. Oil on canvas, 18¼" x 39¼."

12. *Boats on the Seine.* c.1880. Oil on canvas, 10 × 19⅝".
J. P. L. Fine Arts, London

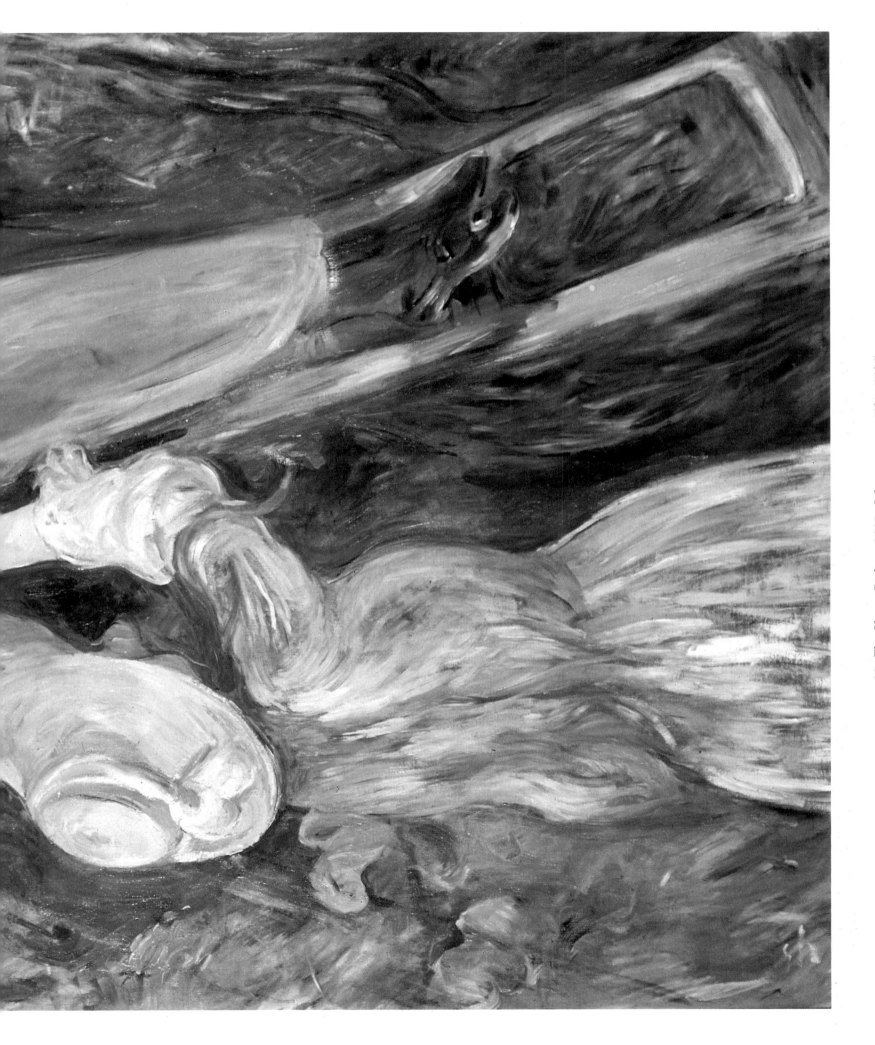

13. *The Cherry Pickers.* 1891. Oil on canvas, 60⅝ × 33⅜".
Private collection, Paris. Giraudon/Art Resource, New York